The Sermon on the Mount:

From Hearing to Doing

By Clay Gentry

Published by
Spiritbuilding Publishers
9700 Ferry Road, Waynesville, Ohio 45068

THE SERMON ON THE MOUNT:
From Hearing to Doing
By Clay Gentry

ISBN: 978–1–964–80542–9

Spiritbuilding
PUBLISHERS
spiritbuilding.com

Table of Contents

Introduction

The Sermon on the Mount:
From Hearing to Doing

Imagine a profound teaching, so concise it can be read in mere minutes, yet so rich and expansive that it can be studied for a lifetime. This is the paradoxical power of the Sermon on the Mount. Often regarded as the very heart of Jesus' teachings—the embodiment of the "gospel of the kingdom." More than a set of abstract ideals, this sermon is a dynamic call to move beyond mere understanding and actively embrace a life transformed by God's truth.

The context for this monumental discourse is crucial. Immediately after His baptism and the temptation in the wilderness (Matthew 3:13–4:11), Jesus began to proclaim His revolutionary message: the good news that the kingdom of God was now on the threshold (Matthew 4:12–25). The Sermon on the Mount, then, is to be seen as the detailed articulation of this kingdom. It spells out the radical repentance and profound righteousness that are not just intellectually grasped, but demanded and demonstrated by those who belong to this new kingdom.

This sermon offers the most comprehensive description in the New Testament of the Christian counterculture—a way of life fundamentally distinct from the world's norms. Critics often dismiss its ideals as noble but impractical, suggesting they are beyond the reach of anyone. However, such a view misses the very purpose of Jesus' sermon: to equip His followers with the righteousness demanded by His Kingdom, guiding them not just to know His words, but to live them out. This transformative journey from hearing to doing is precisely what we will explore in this study. Jesus' teachings are indeed attainable, for it is through the empowering presence of God's grace that we are enabled to live out His radical call. This divine enablement aligns perfectly with Paul's exhortation to "work out your own salvation with fear and trembling, for it is God who works in you, both to will and to work for his good pleasure" (Philippians 2:12–13; cf. Hebrews 13:20–21), underscoring that our obedience flows from His work within us.

This Bible study, "The Sermon on the Mount: From Hearing to Doing," is therefore far more than an intellectual exercise. It's a vital invitation to encounter Jesus, the Son of God, and to allow His living words to profoundly transform us from passive hearers into active doers of His will. As James, the brother of Jesus, powerfully warns us: "But be doers of the word, and not hearers only" (James 1:22). This timeless admonition is the very heart of this study, reminding us that true faith is not merely about accumulating knowledge, but about actively obeying and living out Christ's transformative teachings.
Here's how our journey will unfold:

- Immerse: Start by reading the selected passages from the Sermon on the Mount, reflecting on the words and letting them speak to your heart.
- Reflect: Engage with thought-provoking questions that spark self-examination and challenge your perspectives. Delve into Jesus' teachings and discover their application to our lives.
- Respond: Conclude each lesson with a prayer prompt, an invitation to pour out your heart to God, seeking His

guidance, forgiveness, and the power of His grace in your life, that you might truly live out what you have learned.

As we embark on this study together, may our hearts be open to the profound lessons that await us, and may our lives be significantly transformed by our encounter with God's word. Those who first heard Jesus' sermon were astonished. I pray that you, too, will be astonished and challenged by the greatest sermon ever preached. We will begin by exploring Lesson #1: The Authority Behind the Sermon (Matthew 5:1; 7:28-29), recognizing that the lasting impact of these words resides not just in their content but in the person of Jesus Christ, the one who spoke them with unmatched authority.

Lesson 1

The Authority Behind the Sermon
(5:1; 7:28–29)

The Sermon on the Mount is the pinnacle of spiritual instruction, a discourse that has been etched into the annals of human history. Countless scholars, theologians, and believers have dissected its verses, analyzed its nuances, and pondered its implications. Yet, despite centuries of scrutiny, its message continues to challenge and inspire, offering profound wisdom for contemporary Christians. The enduring power of this sermon resides not merely in its eloquent words but in the person who delivered it: Jesus Christ, the Son of God, the ultimate teacher.

Before we explore this timeless message, let's transport ourselves to the scene depicted in Matthew 5:1; 7:28–29, envisioning the setting, the anticipation, and the awe surrounding Jesus' profound discourse.

Encountering the Teacher and His Teachings

Now, let's delve into the heart of the Sermon on the Mount, examining its message and the authority behind it:

1. **A Scene of Anticipation:** Imagine the scene described in Matthew 5:1. Picture the diverse crowd gathered on the hillside, their faces reflecting a mixture of curiosity and

expectation. What sights, sounds, and even smells might have filled the air that day?

How would you have felt as a member of that audience, eager to hear the words of this renowned teacher?

2. **The Qualities of a Master Teacher:** In your opinion, what qualities make Jesus the greatest teacher of all time?

    Consider specific examples from His ministry that showcase His teaching abilities, profound wisdom, and ability to connect with His audience.

3. **Beyond Mere Teacher:** Imagine a friend or colleague expressing admiration for Jesus only as a great teacher, while overlooking His divine nature and redemptive mission. How would you engage in a conversation that gently guides them toward a deeper understanding of Jesus' identity as the Son of God and the Savior of the world?

4. **The Challenge of Discipleship:** As you reflect on the Sermon on the Mount, which teachings appear most challenging to apply in your life?

    Why should you embrace these instructions as good news despite their difficulty?

5. **The Weight of Authority:** Matthew 7:28–29 highlights the crowd's astonishment at Jesus' teaching, noting that He taught with an authority that surpassed the religious leaders of His time. In what ways is Jesus' authority displayed in the Sermon on the Mount?

Where else in the gospel of Matthew do you find evidence of His divine power, unique insight, and unwavering conviction?

6. **Authority and Relevance:** How does acknowledging Jesus' authority shape your understanding of His teachings and your readiness to incorporate them into your life?

Embracing the Timeless Message

The Sermon on the Mount continues to resonate across the centuries, offering profound wisdom and challenging believers to a higher standard of discipleship. By recognizing the authority behind the message, we can approach these teachings with a renewed sense of reverence and commitment, allowing them to shape our lives and draw us closer to the heart of Christ.

Prayer Prompt: Lord, as I begin to study Your Son's Sermon on the Mount, open my heart to His authority, teachings, and transforming power.

Lesson 2

Unveiling True Blessedness

O ur culture often equates blessedness with material prosperity, good health, and a life free from adversity. Yet, Jesus, in His profound wisdom, challenges this conventional notion, presenting a radically different perspective on what it means to be truly blessed. He unveils a paradox: true blessedness is often found in brokenness, humility, and a willingness to embrace suffering for the sake of righteousness. This is the narrow path of discipleship, a path that diverges from the broad road pursued by those seeking worldly comfort and acclaim.

Before we delve into the depths of Jesus' teachings, let's revisit the Beatitudes in Matthew 5:2–12, allowing His words to challenge our preconceptions and reshape our understanding of true blessedness.

Embracing the Paradox of Blessedness

Now, let's explore the counter-cultural wisdom embedded in the Beatitudes:

1. **Redefining Blessedness:** Jesus' teachings immediately challenge preconceived notions of what it means to be truly happy or blessed. What characteristics or circumstances typically come to mind when you think of a blessed or fortunate person?

How does your perception diverge from Jesus' definition of blessedness?

2. **The Beatitudes Inverted:** To gain a fresh perspective on these familiar verses, consider rephrasing them from an opposite point of view. For example, reword v. 3 as, "Woe to the arrogant, for theirs is the kingdom of hell."

What insights emerge when you examine the Beatitudes from this contrasting angle?

3. **A Progression of Qualities:** Starting with the first beatitude, "Blessed are the poor in spirit" (v. 3), trace the progression of characteristics that Jesus attributes to the truly blessed. How does each quality build upon the previous one, culminating in a portrait of a person who embodies the heart and spirit of Christ?

4. **Personal Resonance:** Choose one or two Beatitudes that stand out to you. In your own words, elaborate on what you believe Jesus is conveying in that statement.

How does this particular declaration of "blessedness" reshape your understanding of authentic spiritual well-being?

5. **The Cost of Discipleship:** Verse 11 stands out as the only beatitude that receives further commentary. Why would the world persecute and hate those who embody the qualities described in the Beatitudes?

What does this reveal about the cost of discipleship and the inherent conflict between the values of the Kingdom of God and the values of the world?

6. **A Personal Inventory:** Reflect on your own life and spiritual journey. Which qualities from the Beatitudes do you most need to cultivate at this stage?

What steps can you take to embrace the paradox of blessedness, recognizing that true fulfillment often lies in humility, dependence on God, and a willingness to endure suffering for righteousness' sake?

The Path to True Blessedness

The Beatitudes challenge us to reevaluate our understanding of blessedness. They recognize that true fulfillment is not found in worldly success or comfort but in aligning our lives with the values of God's Kingdom. By embracing the qualities described by Jesus, we embark on a path that leads to genuine blessedness, both in this life and in the life to come.

Prayer Prompt: Lord, challenge my worldly understanding of blessedness. Open my eyes to your definition revealed in the Beatitudes, especially where it contrasts with my own desires for comfort and ease.

Lesson 3

Salt and Light in a World of Darkness

In a world where many may never open a Bible, Christians become the living embodiment of the Gospel message. Our actions, attitudes, and relationships shape the perceptions of those around us, communicating volumes about the God we serve. As the hymn aptly states, "We are the only Bibles the careless world will read." This profound responsibility calls us to be both salt and light, influencing our communities and reflecting the transformative power of God's grace.

Before we delve into the specific metaphors of salt and light, let's ground ourselves in Matthew 5:13-16, allowing Jesus' words to illuminate our understanding of our role in the world.

Embracing Our Influence

Now, let's explore the practical implications of being salt and light in a world shrouded in darkness:

1. **Salt of the Earth:** Jesus declares, "You are the salt of the earth" (v. 13). In ancient times, salt served both as a preservative and a flavor enhancer. How does this metaphor illuminate the Christian's role in society?

What aspects of our world need preservation and seasoning?

2. **Losing Our Saltiness:** What factors or behaviors can diminish a Christian's "saltiness," rendering them ineffective in influencing their surroundings?

   How can we guard against these pitfalls and maintain our distinctiveness as agents of preservation and transformation?

3. **Light of the World:** Jesus continues, "You are the light of the world" (v. 14). Complete the following sentence with as many words as possible: "In a world darkened by sin, Christians are to serve as a light of _____."

4. **Hiding Our Light:** Identify any temptations or fears that might lead Christians to hide their light, preventing it from shining brightly in the world.

   How can we overcome these obstacles and boldly illuminate the path toward God's grace?

5. **A Convincing Testimony:** How can a life characterized by the qualities described in the Beatitudes, coupled with the influence of salt and light, serve as a compelling testament to the saving power of God?

   In what ways do our actions and attitudes enhance the credibility of our message?

6. **Expanding Our Influence:** Brainstorm practical and creative ways to amplify your collective and individual impact as salt and light within your communities.

How can you actively engage in preserving truth, enhancing the lives of others, and illuminating the path toward God's redemptive love?

Shining Brightly in the Darkness

As salt and light, Christians are called to be agents of preservation, flavor, and illumination in a world that is desperately in need of God's transforming grace. By embracing our roles as influencers, we can actively participate in God's redemptive work, drawing others toward the light of His love and demonstrating the power of the Gospel to transform lives.

Prayer Prompt: Lord, help me grasp my role as salt and light. Show me how to be a preserving, flavorful influence for Your gospel. Grant me the courage to shine Your light brightly in darkness, so others see Your goodness through me.

Lesson 4

Unveiling the Heart's Hidden Depths

J esus, in His profound wisdom, challenges us to look beyond outward actions and delve into the hidden depths of the human heart. He exposes the subtle sins that often lurk beneath the surface, which can erode our relationship with God and hinder our spiritual growth. In this passage, He confronts the destructive power of anger and lust, revealing their insidious nature and urging us to pursue purity of heart and mind.

Before we explore the depths of these challenging teachings, let's immerse ourselves in Matthew 5:17–30, allowing Jesus' words to penetrate our hearts and illuminate the path to true righteousness.

Confronting the Sins Within

Now, let's delve into Jesus' teachings on anger and lust, and examine their implications for our lives:

1. **The Foundation of the Law:** Imagine a world without the Old Testament. What essential truths about God, humanity, and the nature of sin would be missing from our understanding?

How does the Old Testament lay the groundwork for Jesus' teachings and the fulfillment of God's redemptive plan?

2. **Fulfilling the Law:** Jesus emphatically declares that He did not come to abolish the Law but to fulfill it. Why does He stress this point?

   How does His life and ministry demonstrate the true essence and purpose of the Law?

3. **The Spectrum of Anger:** Jesus places murder, unrighteous anger, and insulting language on the same spectrum of sin. Do you view these actions as equally destructive? Explain.

   How are they interconnected, and what do they reveal about the state of our hearts?

4. **The Urgency of Reconciliation:** Jesus emphasizes the importance of swift reconciliation and apology (v. 25). Reflect on a time when you either initiated forgiveness or experienced someone seeking forgiveness from you. What was the outcome of that encounter?

   How did forgiveness impact your relationship and your own spiritual well-being?

5. **The Struggle with Lust:** Jesus employs graphic language in verses 29-30 to underscore the seriousness of lust. Why do we find it so challenging to "amputate" those things that cause us to stumble spiritually?

    What practical steps can we take to guard our hearts and minds against the allure of lust?

6. **Cultivating Purity:** This passage focuses on maintaining spiritual and mental purity. What kinds of meditation and reflection can help us cultivate and safeguard this purity?

    How can we fill our minds with thoughts that nourish our souls and draw us closer to God?

The Path to Inner Transformation

Jesus' teachings on anger and lust challenge us to confront the hidden depths of our hearts, recognizing the subtle sins that can hinder our spiritual growth. By pursuing purity of heart and mind, actively seeking reconciliation, and guarding against temptation, we can cultivate a life that reflects the true righteousness exemplified by Christ.

Prayer Prompt: Lord, search my heart and reveal any roots of anger or lust that are festering within. Give me the strength to acknowledge these hidden sins and the willingness to surrender them to Your transforming grace.

Lesson 5

The Foundation of Marriage: Fidelity and Truth-Telling

F ew experiences rival the anguish of a broken marriage, a bond intended for love and companionship that dissolves into bitterness and discord. In this passage, Jesus addresses fidelity and the importance of truthful speech, two threads intricately woven into the fabric of marriage. He challenges us to uphold the integrity of our commitments, recognizing that our words and actions reflect on ourselves and the God we represent.

Before we explore the depths of Jesus' teachings, let's listen closely to Matthew 5:31-37 and allow His words to guide us toward a deeper understanding of fidelity and truth-telling in marriage and speech.

Honoring Our Commitments

Now, let's examine the practical implications of Jesus' teachings:

1. **The Erosion of Commitment:** The anguish of a broken marriage is an unfortunate reality in our world today. Before we delve into Jesus' specific teachings on fidelity, from your perspective, what are the top reasons marriages falter and ultimately fail?

How do these factors contribute to the breakdown of trust, communication, and intimacy within a marriage relationship?

2. **Redefining Divorce:** In Matthew 19:7, the Pharisees cite Moses' instructions on divorce as a "command" (Deuteronomy 24:1–4), believing that adhering to the letter of the law equates to righteousness. How does Jesus' response challenge their legalistic interpretation and illuminate the true meaning and implications of divorce (Matthew 5:31–32; 19:3–9)?

3. **Oaths and Marital Fidelity:** The Pharisees had developed elaborate formulas for oaths, distinguishing between binding and non-binding pronouncements. How do oaths and vows relate to marriage and divorce?

4. **Integrity as a Witness:** Jesus' teaching on oaths is not a blanket prohibition but a call to cultivate integrity and truthfulness in all our interactions. How does a Christian's commitment to honesty reflect on Christ and the church?

How might dishonesty hinder the spread of the Gospel and undermine our witness to the world?

5. **Unfulfilled Promises:** Recall any "I promise" commitments you've made recently—perhaps to your spouse, children, friend, church, colleague, etc.—that remain unfulfilled.

Now take a moment to write down the steps necessary to make amends, outlining how and when you will fulfill those neglected promises.

6. **A Marital Inventory:** If you are married, revisit the vows exchanged with your spouse. Have you remained faithful to those promises? In what areas do you need to strengthen your commitment and renew your efforts to honor your marriage covenant?

The Foundation of Trust

Faithfulness in marriage and honesty in speech are essential for building trust and reflecting the character of God. By upholding the sanctity of our commitments and speaking truthfully in all circumstances, we reveal the transformative power of the Gospel and lay a solid foundation for healthy relationships and effective ministry.

Prayer Prompt: Lord, empower me to honor my marriage and develop the integrity to speak truth, reflecting Your character in all my relationships and conversations.

Lesson 6

Embracing Radical Love

The true measure of love lies not in our affection for the amiable but in our response to the antagonistic. Jesus, in His radical teachings, calls us to transcend the natural inclination toward retaliation and embrace a love that extends even to our enemies. This counter-cultural ethic, far from being mere practical wisdom, reflects the very heart of God, setting His followers apart as beacons of compassion in a world often driven by animosity and strife.

Before we delve into the challenging implications of this teaching, let's hear Jesus' words in Matthew 5:38-48, allowing them to penetrate our hearts and reshape our understanding of love.

Transcending Retaliation

Now, let's explore the practical dimensions of loving our enemies:

1. **The Difficulty of Love:** Jesus' call to love our enemies and transcend retaliation is arguably one of His most radical and challenging commands. Let's begin by honestly reflecting on its difficulty: What aspects of His instructions in these verses do you find most challenging to embrace?

What deeply ingrained human tendencies and cultural norms make extending love to those who have hurt or offended you difficult?

2. **Misapplication of Justice:** The Pharisees distorted the judicial principle of "an eye for an eye" by applying it to personal relationships. What potential consequences arise when one adopts a mindset of equal retribution and retaliation in our interactions with others?

When are you most tempted to respond in kind when someone wrongs you? Why?

3. **Natural vs. Supernatural Responses:** In vv. 39–42, Jesus contrasts our instinctive reactions to aggression with the responses He expects from His followers. How do these contrasting approaches reflect the difference between a worldly mindset and a Christ-centered perspective?

4. **Love, Not Passivity:** Loving our enemies doesn't mean that Christians should become passive doormats, allowing others to exploit or mistreat them. Clarify how genuine love can coexist with healthy boundaries and assertive communication.

5. **Transformative Love:** When faced with an enemy, how can acts of love—turning the other cheek, generously giving, going the extra mile, expressing affection, and praying fervently—impact both your heart and the heart of your adversary (cf. Romans 12:14–21)?

   How can such actions break down barriers, foster understanding, and potentially lead to reconciliation?

6. **Extending the Hand of Love:** Identify someone you consider an enemy or who has treated you unkindly. This week, make a conscious effort to pray for this person and extend a practical gesture of love toward them. Reflect on how this act of obedience shapes your perspective and potentially opens doors for healing and reconciliation.

Love's Transforming Power

Loving our enemies serves as a radical testament to the transformative power of the Gospel. By embracing this counter-cultural ethic, we not only reflect the heart of God but also become agents of reconciliation and healing in a world fractured by conflict and animosity.

Prayer Prompt: Lord, train me with Your grace to love my enemies, moving beyond retaliation to embrace radical love. Show me practical ways to extend mercy, reflecting Your own heart in this world.

Lesson 7

Unmasking the Heart of True Religion

W hile the call to resist worldly conformity resonates throughout the New Testament (cf. Romans 12:1–2), Jesus also cautioned against conforming to the outward trappings of religious piety. He recognized the seductive allure of self-centered religiosity and challenged His followers to cultivate an authentic faith that transcends mere external rituals.

Before we delve into Jesus' teachings on genuine piety, let's take note of Matthew 6:1–18 and allow His words to expose the subtle hypocrisy that can infiltrate our religious practices.

Exposing the Counterfeit

Now, let's explore the distinctions between genuine and superficial religious expression:

1. **Righteousness on Display:** In v. 1, Jesus warns against practicing righteousness "before other people in order to be seen by them." Yet, in 5:16, He encourages His followers to "let your light shine before others." How can we reconcile the call to good works with the warning against pretentious displays of piety?

2. **Motives Matter:** Jesus provides examples related to giving, praying, and fasting to illustrate the importance of having proper motives. In your own words, briefly summarize the distinction between genuine and hypocritical actions.

3. **The Temptation of Giving:** In what ways are we tempted to give or share for self-serving reasons instead of from a pure desire to honor God and meet the needs of others?

   How can we cultivate a spirit of generosity that rises above the need for recognition or personal gain?

4. **Authentic Prayer:** Jesus continues His unmasking of counterfeit piety by turning His attention to prayer. How should our prayers differ from the hypocritical displays of the Pharisees and the repetitive chants of the pagans?

   What qualities define a genuine, intimate prayer life that prioritizes seeking God's will above all else?

5. **The Significance of Fasting:** Though less emphasized or even absent in some modern churches, fasting is nevertheless presented by Jesus as another key indicator of true religious authenticity. In what ways do His teachings on the topic apply to your life and your congregation (cf. Acts 13:1–2; 14:23)?

What spiritual benefits can be gained from incorporating fasting into your spiritual disciplines?

6. **Cultivating Authenticity:** Reflect on your spiritual practices. What changes can you make to foster a more authentic faith, particularly in the realms of giving, prayer, and fasting?

How can you ensure that your outward actions align with the true desires of your heart?

Beyond Outward Appearances

Jesus' teachings in Matthew 6:1–18 challenge us to move beyond superficial religious practices and cultivate a faith that is deeply rooted in sincerity and humility. By examining our motives, prioritizing genuine devotion over outward displays, and embracing practices such as fasting, we can cultivate a vibrant and authentic relationship with God that permeates every aspect of our lives.

Prayer Prompt: Lord, examine my heart, revealing any selfish motives in my giving, praying, fasting, and any other devotion. Forgive these desires and purify me, so that all I do flows from genuine love and a desire to honor You.

Lesson 8

The Heart of Prayer

P rayer, at its core, is a dialogue with God, an expression of our relationship with Him. Yet, the nature of our prayers often reflects our underlying perception of God. Hypocrites approach God with insincerity, seeking the applause of others rather than genuine communion. Pagans, trapped in a cycle of empty repetition, view God as a reluctant giver who must be coerced through incessant pleas. In stark contrast, Jesus invites His followers into a relationship with a loving Father who knows our needs before we even utter them. The Lord's Prayer serves as a model, guiding us toward a prayer life characterized by reverence, trust, and a deep understanding of God's character.

Before we delve into the depths of Jesus' teachings on prayer, let's combine Matthew 6:5–15 and 7:7–11, allowing His words to shape our approach to communicating with our Heavenly Father.

Transforming Our Prayer Life

Now, let's delve into the principles that underpin authentic prayer:

1. **Beyond Empty Words:** Having highlighted prayer as the core of our relationship with God, Jesus immediately draws a glaring contrast between prayers driven by performance or repetition and those rooted in a genuine relationship. What

distinguishes a prayer that comes from a deep relationship with God from one that seeks only outward appearances or personal gain?

2. **The Purpose of Prayer:** If, as Jesus states in verse 8, "your Father knows what you need before you ask Him," why should Christians engage in prayer?

   Beyond merely presenting our requests, what other relational, transformative, or worshipful purposes does prayer serve?

3. **A Model for Prayer:** Take your time to meditate on each phrase of the Lord's Prayer. How does this model challenge and refine your own approach to prayer?

   In what ways can you more closely align your prayers with the pattern Jesus provides?

4. **The Power of Forgiveness:** Jesus emphasizes the vital role forgiveness plays in the believer's prayer life (vv. 14–15). Reflect on a time when your prayers were obstructed by unforgiveness in your heart. How did extending forgiveness to others, just as God has forgiven you, affect your relationship with God and your prayer life?

5. **Perseverance in Prayer:** The Christian life is often filled with challenges and setbacks. What encouragement does Jesus offer to those who continually ask, seek, and knock through prayer?

   How does His teaching inspire us to persevere in prayer, even when confronted with apparent delays or unanswered requests?

6. **The Father's Heart:** As you reflect on Jesus' instructions about prayer and His call to ask, seek, and knock, what image emerges of our Heavenly Father?

   How does this understanding of God's character empower and transform your prayer life?

A Deeper Connection

Jesus' teachings on prayer invite us into a deeper, more intimate relationship with our Heavenly Father. By embracing the principles of authenticity, humility, forgiveness, and persistence, we can cultivate a prayer life that reflects the heart of true discipleship and draws us closer to the source of all wisdom and grace.

Prayer Prompt: Lord, examine my prayer life. Reveal any tendencies to perform or empty repetition. Teach me genuine connection where my words are few, but my heart is fully engaged. Help me seek Your will and presence above all else.

Lesson 9

Where Your Treasure Is

In a world obsessed with material possessions, Jesus challenges us to reconsider where we place our trust and invest our hearts. He exposes the fleeting nature of earthly treasures and contrasts them with the enduring riches of the Kingdom of God. This passage invites us to make a fundamental choice: Will we chase after fleeting possessions and succumb to worry, or will we seek first God's Kingdom and experience the peace that transcends all understanding?

Before we delve into the depths of Jesus' teaching, let's engage with Matthew 6:19–34, allowing His words to reorient our priorities and liberate us from the shackles of anxiety.

The Choice Before Us

Now, let's explore the implications of Jesus' teachings on treasure and worry:

1. **Treasures, Eyes, and Masters:** In vv. 19–24, Jesus connects the concepts of treasures, eyes, and masters. Identify unifying themes or principles that tie these seemingly disparate elements together.

   How do they illuminate the choices we make regarding our ultimate allegiance and priorities?

2. **Escaping the Grip of Worry:** Worry dominates vv. 25–34. What fundamental shift in perspective does He call for to alleviate our fears and cultivate trust in God's provision?

3. **The Evolution of Worry:** While Jesus addresses concerns about basic needs, our modern anxieties often extend beyond food and clothing. What contemporary worries might replace these fundamental concerns?

    Reflect on your own list of potential anxieties. Has worry ever yielded a positive outcome or resolved any of these concerns?

4. **The Impact of Our Choices:** How do the pivotal choices we make regarding our treasures and priorities (vv. 19–24, 33) influence our ability to live free from the burdens of worry and anxiety?

    In what ways does seeking first God's Kingdom provide a foundation for peace and contentment, even amidst life's uncertainties?

5. **Discerning When to Worry:** While Jesus discourages worry over necessities, there are instances where concern and thoughtful consideration are warranted (i.e., 1 Corinthians 7:32–33; 2 Corinthians 11:28). How can we discern between anxieties that hinder our faith and legitimate concerns that require our attention and action?

6. **Confronting Our Anxieties:** Share one of your current worries with the group. Discuss how Jesus' teachings can be specifically applied to your situation to ease your anxiety and cultivate trust in God's provision and sovereignty.

The Path to Peace

Jesus' teachings on treasure and worry challenge us to re-evaluate our priorities and place our trust in the enduring riches of God's Kingdom. By seeking first His will and acknowledging His sovereign care, we can break free from the shackles of anxiety and experience the true peace that surpasses all understanding.

Prayer Prompt: Lord, forgive me for when my worries and lack of trust in You take over my heart. Teach me to trust You with tomorrow and find peace in Your unfailing love today.

Lesson 10

The Peril of Judgment

The church, ideally, should be a sanctuary of support, a community where individuals uplift one another, nurture their relationships with God, and extend a welcoming hand to those seeking Christ. However, the intrusion of self-righteousness can transform this haven into a place of condemnation, manipulation, and indifference. Jesus, in His wisdom, confronts the destructive nature of judgmental attitudes, recognizing their potential to erode relationships and impede the advancement of the Gospel.

Before we explore the depths of Jesus' teaching, let's seriously consider Matthew 7:1–6, allowing His words to challenge our perspectives and guide us toward a more compassionate and discerning approach to others.

Removing the Plank from Our Own Eye

Now, let's delve into the implications of Jesus' caution against judgment:

1. **The Call to Mercy:** To address the peril of judgment, Jesus immediately confronts His followers with a powerful imperative: "Judge not, that you be not judged" (v. 1). Let's consider the depth of this command: Why does Jesus explicitly instruct us to refrain from judging others?

How do these verses expand upon His earlier teaching in the Beatitudes regarding the importance of extending mercy?

What connection does He draw between receiving mercy and showing mercy to others?

2. **The Blind Leading the Blind:** Jesus warns of the danger of attempting to guide others spiritually while remaining oblivious to our own shortcomings. What consequences might arise when we adopt a judgmental posture without addressing our own areas of weakness?

How can this lead to hypocrisy and spiritual blindness?

3. **Discernment vs. Judgment:** Articulate the distinction between judging others and exercising proper discernment. How can we evaluate the actions and beliefs of others with wisdom and compassion, avoiding the pitfalls of condemnation and self-righteousness?

4. **Protecting the Sacred:** In the context of evangelism, in what ways can we heed Jesus' warning against giving "dogs" what is sacred or throwing "pearls" to "pigs"?

How can we faithfully discern when it's time to move on from those who are antagonistic to the gospel and you?

5. **The Scars of Judgment:** Summarize a situation where you witnessed a relationship, either within the church or outside of it, damaged by a Christian's judgmental attitude.

In what ways did this behavior contradict Jesus' teachings and hinder the expression of God's love and grace?

6. **The Fruit of Restraint:** If you consistently applied Jesus' guidelines on judging others, what positive and negative effects might you anticipate in your relationships?

How could this shift in perspective foster greater understanding, compassion, and unity within the body of Christ and beyond?

A Call to Humility and Grace

Jesus' teachings on judgment serve as a potent reminder of our own need for grace and the importance of extending that same grace to others. By cultivating humility, practicing discernment, and prioritizing restoration over condemnation, we can create a community characterized by love, acceptance, and the transformative power of the Gospel.

Prayer Prompt: Lord, help me to examine my own heart first, removing the "plank" from my eye. Cultivate in me a spirit of mercy and compassion, guiding me to discern wisely without falling into self-righteous condemnation.

Lesson 11

Living the Golden Rule

The Sermon on the Mount, a treasure trove of timeless wisdom, has gifted the world with numerous phrases that have become ingrained in our collective vocabulary: "go the extra mile," "don't hide your light under a bushel," "a city on a hill," "salt of the earth," "the narrow gate." Yet perhaps no teaching shines brighter than the Golden Rule: "Do to others what you would have them do to you" (Matthew 7:12). This simple yet profound principle, if genuinely embraced, can transform our interactions, unlock opportunities to demonstrate Jesus' love, and enrich our relationships.

Before we explore the implications of this timeless teaching, take a moment to slowly read the familiar words of Matthew 7:12, allowing its wisdom to resonate within your heart and guide your actions.

Beyond Reciprocity

Now, let's explore the depths of the Golden Rule and its practical application in our lives:

1. **Early Encounters:** Perhaps no teaching from the Sermon on the Mount is as universally recognized or ingrained in our culture as the Golden Rule. To begin, reflect on your earliest memory of encountering the Golden Rule. Who introduced you to this principle, and how did it shape your understanding of treating others?

2. **A Higher Standard:** Variations of the Golden Rule existed before Jesus, for example, Rabbi Hillel taught, "What is hateful to yourself, do not do to your neighbor." Evaluate the nature and implications of this 'negative' formulation of the rule.

   In contrast, how does Jesus' teaching, particularly as vividly illustrated in the Parable of the Good Samaritan (Luke 10:25–37), compel us beyond mere avoidance of harm toward a more proactive and compassionate engagement with others?

3. **The Essence of the Law:** Jesus reveals this simple rule to be the heart of all God's commands and prophetic teachings. In what sense does the Golden Rule embody the essence of the Law and the Prophets?

   How does this relate to the broader teachings of the Sermon on the Mount as a unifying principle for righteous living?

4. **Obstacles to Application:** What obstacles hinder our consistent application of the Golden Rule? With whom and in what situations are you most tempted to ignore Jesus' teaching on treating others as you would like to be treated?

   What internal barriers or external pressures lead to this inconsistency?

5. **Modeling the Desired Behavior:** How do you wish to be treated by your spouse, coworker, neighbor, friend, or even your enemy? Are you actively showing that same treatment toward them?

Offer specific examples of how to embody the Golden Rule in your different relationships.

6. **Mending Broken Bridges:** Reflect on a relationship that is currently strained or fractured. How can applying the Golden Rule contribute to healing and reconciliation in this relationship?

What steps can you take this week to initiate the restoration process, guided by the principle of treating others as you would like to be treated?

A Universal Principle

The Golden Rule, a timeless principle with universal appeal, invites us to move beyond self-centeredness and adopt a way of living defined by empathy, compassion, and genuine concern for the well-being of others. By actively applying this teaching in our daily interactions, we can transform our relationships, reflect the love of Christ, and contribute to a more harmonious and just world.

Prayer Prompt: Lord, move me beyond merely avoiding harm to a proactive love. Show me where I falter and empower me to consistently apply this principle in all my relationships, reflecting your compassionate heart.

Lesson 12

Navigating the Crossroads of Truth

As He concludes His Sermon on the Mount, Jesus presents His followers with a stark choice, a spiritual crossroads. He contrasts the broad, well-traveled path leading to destruction with the narrow, often difficult path that leads to life. This decision requires discernment, an awareness of the deceptive allure of the world's lies, and a firm commitment to the unwavering truth of God's Kingdom.

Before we examine the implications of this pivotal choice, let's read Matthew 7:13–20, letting Jesus' words illuminate the path and guide us toward the narrow gate.

Choosing the Narrow Way

Now, let's delve into the challenges and rewards of following the narrow path:

1. **The Narrow Gate:** As Jesus brings His sermon to a close, He presents His followers with a pivotal choice—the broad way and the narrow way. What makes the gate of Christianity "small" and the road "narrow"?

   Identify any inherent challenges and sacrifices that come with embracing a life of discipleship and rejecting the broad way.

2. **Obstacles on the Path:** What specific obstacles hinder your progress on the narrow path? Write down your top two or three challenges and prayerfully consider how to overcome them with God's grace and strength.

3. **The Allure of Deception:** Why do broad gates and false prophets hold such appeal in today's world?

   What underlying desires or societal influences contribute to the widespread acceptance of deceptive ideologies and compromised values?

4. **Explaining the Narrow Way:** Imagine having a conversation with an unbelieving friend about the blessings of the "narrow way" of Christ. How would you express the essence of Jesus' teaching in a clear, compelling, and compassionate way?

5. **Discerning the Fruit:** Jesus instructs us to recognize false prophets "by their fruits" (v. 16a). What kinds of fruit does He have in mind?

How can we evaluate the quality of a person's life and teachings to determine their alignment with God's truth?

6. **The Warning of Complacency:** Jesus warns that every tree that fails to bear good fruit will be cut down and thrown into the fire (v. 19). How does this warning, primarily directed toward false prophets, also act as a caution against complacency for Christians?

How can it inspire us to remain vigilant in our faith and actively seek spiritual growth?

Walking in Truth

Jesus' closing words in the Sermon on the Mount challenge us to choose wisely, embrace the narrow path that leads to life, and remain discerning in a world filled with deceptive voices. By cultivating a deep understanding of God's truth and actively pursuing a life marked by genuine faith and good works, we can navigate the crossroads with confidence and walk steadfastly toward the Kingdom of God.

Prayer Prompt: Lord, led me to choose the narrow gate to life. Grant me discernment to resist deception and false prophets. Empower me to bear good fruit as I walk steadfastly in Your truth.

Lesson 13

The Ultimate Choice

The culmination of the Sermon on the Mount presents us with the most consequential decision of our lives: how will we respond to Jesus? This choice goes beyond career paths, relationships, or any other worldly pursuits. It determines our eternal destiny. Jesus contrasts two starkly different responses to His teachings, emphasizing that neutrality is an illusion. We must choose. Will we embrace His words and build our lives upon their unshakable foundation, or will we disregard them and face the inevitable consequences?

Before we explore the implications of this ultimate choice, let's listen as Jesus concludes with Matthew 7:21–27, letting His words shape our eternal trajectory.

Building on the Rock

Now, let's delve into the contrasting responses to Jesus' message:

1. **The Illusion of Piety:** On the surface, the individuals described in verses 21–23 seem devout and impressive. They prophesy, cast out demons, and perform miracles in Jesus' name. Yet, He ultimately condemns them. Why?

    What does Jesus' condemnation of these seemingly devout individuals teach us about the critical distinction between outward religious acts and an authentic relationship with Him?

2. **Activity vs. Obedience:** Why do people often confuse religious busyness with genuine obedience to God's will?

What subtle motivations or cultural pressures do you think contribute to this misunderstanding?

How can we ensure that our actions are grounded in genuine devotion rather than in a desire for recognition or self-justification?

3. **The Revealing Storms:** Jesus emphasizes the challenge of distinguishing between genuine and counterfeit followers of Christ. How do the storms of life—trials, temptations, and adversity—reveal the true foundation of a person's faith?

What qualities are revealed in those who have based their lives on the solid rock of Christ?

4. **The Obedience of Faith:** Jesus compares obedience to His teachings to building a house upon a rock. How does this metaphor illustrate the stability and security that come from aligning our lives with His words?

What are the practical implications of applying His teachings?

5. **Weathering the Storms:** Reflect on the storms you have faced in your life. What trials, temptations, or adversities have challenged the foundation of your faith?

What do these experiences reveal about the sincerity of your commitment to Christ?

6. **The Cost of Discipleship:** Putting Jesus' words into practice requires intentionality and sacrifice. What specific demands might living out the principles of the Sermon on the Mount place on your life?

What areas might need reevaluation, repentance, or renewed commitment?

The Foundation of Eternity

The closing verses of the Sermon on the Mount present us with a stark choice: to build on the sand of empty religiosity or on the rock of obedience to Christ. This decision has eternal ramifications. By embracing His teachings and actively applying them in our lives, we lay a foundation that will withstand the storms of life and the scrutiny of the final judgment.

Prayer Prompt: Lord, Your final words in the Sermon on the Mount confront me with the ultimate choice. Help me truly obey Your teachings, not just hear them, and build my life upon Your unshakeable truth. May my faith be genuine, tested by life's storms, so that I stand firm on the rock of Christ.

A Note from the Author

It's only right that I thank those who helped me bring this study, "The Sermon on the Mount: From Hearing to Doing," to life. First and foremost, I'm deeply grateful to the Jackson Heights Church of Christ for entrusting me with the privilege of dedicating my life to the preaching and teaching of God's word. Special thanks are due to the adults and high school students who participated in the early versions of these lessons. Your thoughtful questions and insights were invaluable for identifying the kinks, helping to ensure this study genuinely guides participants from hearing Jesus' words to putting them into practice.

I would be remiss if I didn't also express my profound gratitude to my incredible wife, Shelly, for her unwavering support and encouragement throughout this process. Her patience, especially in allowing me to work late into the night on these lessons, has been a constant source of strength. She is truly an inspiration, and I could not have completed this study, let alone be the preacher I am, without her.

And finally, a heartfelt thank you to you for journeying through this study with me. The Sermon on the Mount is not merely a collection of moral teachings; it is Jesus' profound declaration of Kingdom life, offering unparalleled insights into true righteousness and what it means to genuinely follow Him. As we delved into its verses, we explored themes of radical love, authentic prayer, true blessedness, and the foundational choices that define our lives, all with the intent of moving us from understanding to action.

So, let me leave you with this exhortation: Go forth from this study, not merely as hearers of Jesus' challenging words, but as doers of them. May you be salt and light in a world desperately in need of God's transforming grace. Embrace the challenging call to seek first His Kingdom and His righteousness, building your life firmly on the unshakeable rock of His teachings. Remember, the Sermon on the Mount is not an impractical ideal, but the very blueprint for abundant life in Christ—a blueprint meant to be built upon, not just read.

I sincerely hope that this study has been a valuable resource for you, deepening your understanding of God's Word and challenging you to live more fully in His Kingdom. If this study has helped you move from hearing to doing, or if you have spiritual questions, I'd love to hear from you. Drop me a line at clay@thebibleway.org, or if you're ever in the Columbia, TN area, let's grab a cup of coffee and talk about Jesus, His Sermon, or anything else on your heart (and maybe a little Elvis, too!).

Thank you again for your participation in this study. May God bless you abundantly as you strive to live out the truths of His Kingdom.

—Clay

P.S. If you enjoyed this study, please consider sharing it with your friends and family. Together, we can spread the transformative message of Jesus' Sermon on the Mount to the world.

How to Lead Your Small Group or Bible Class Through the Sermon on the Mount Study

Welcome, teacher! You're about to embark on a deeply rewarding journey, guiding your group through Jesus' most significant teachings in the Sermon on the Mount. This guide is designed to provide you with practical steps and principles for leading a lively, transformative discussion using this Bible study guide.

As teachers, our goal is not merely to cover content, but to see lives genuinely impacted by God's Word. This inductive study method—Observation, Interpretation, and Application—is a powerful tool for achieving that.

Your Core Responsibilities As a Teacher

Before we dive into the rhythm of each study, understand your essential role:

- **Guide, Don't Lecture:** Your primary task is to facilitate learning, not to deliver a sermon. Resist the urge to share everything you know. Aim for the "70/30 Rule": listen 70% of the time, talk 30%.
- **Cultivate a Safe Space:** Create an environment of trust, respect, and confidentiality where everyone feels comfortable honestly sharing their thoughts and feelings.
- **Keep Christ Central:** Always point back to Jesus as the ultimate authority and the focus of our study.
- **Encourage Participation:** Draw out diverse insights and ensure all voices are heard and valued.

The Study's Flow:
A Step-by-Step Guide

Each lesson in this Sermon on the Mount study guide follows a consistent, inductive pattern. Here's how you'll lead your group through it each week:

—Step 1—
Preparation Is Paramount
(Before the Group Meets)

This is the single most critical step for you as the leader. The more you've personally wrestled with the text, the better you can facilitate.

1. **Read the Lesson Thoroughly:** Read the entire lesson for the week (Introduction, Scripture, Questions, Conclusion, Prayer Prompt) multiple times.

2. **Immerse in the Scripture:** Read the assigned Bible passage (e.g., Matthew 5:2–12 for Lesson #2) at least three to five times—it's helpful to use multiple translations. Pray for understanding.

3. **Answer Every Question:** Go through all six questions in the lesson as if you were a participant. Write down your own observations, interpretations, and applications. Don't skip this step! Your preparation will equip you to gently steer the discussion if it veers off course or to offer a clarifying thought if the group struggles.

4. **Anticipate Discussion:** As you answer, think about:
- Where might the group get stuck?

- Are there any potentially sensitive or controversial points?
- What are the possible different answers or perspectives for each question?
- How might this passage challenge typical assumptions or cultural norms?

5. **Identify Transitions:** Review your written answers and think about how the questions flow from observation to interpretation and then to application. Plan how you'll transition from one question to the next (we'll discuss this more in Step 4).

6. **Pray Specifically:** Pray for each person in your group by name. Pray that the Lord will open hearts and minds, bring clarity to the discussion, and that God will transform lives through His Word.

Encourage Group Member Preparation

Though you can't force it, strongly encourage your group members to read the Scripture and ideally, answer the questions beforehand. This maximizes discussion quality. You might suggest, "Please take some time this week to read Matthew [chapter:verse] and think through questions 1 and 2, so we can hit the ground running."

—Step 2—
Beginning the Session
(The First 5 Minutes)

The first few minutes of your session are crucial for setting a positive and focused atmosphere. Use this time to welcome participants, settle the group, and smoothly transition into the study.

1. **Welcome & Connect:** Greet everyone warmly. Share some small talk to help participants transition from their day and connect. This helps build a safe environment.

2. **Open in prayer (optional):** Ask the Lord to bless your time together. Pray for understanding, humble hearts, and a sincere connection with God's Word. I mention it's optional because each lesson ends with a prayer prompt to close the study.

3. **Read the Introduction:** As the leader, read aloud the "Introduction" for the lesson. Each introduction is designed to "set the stage for the passage" and "prepare minds for the study ahead." This grounds everyone in the context.

4. **Read the Scripture Aloud:** Invite a participant to read the assigned "Scripture Reading" aloud. Encourage them to read slowly and clearly, allowing everyone to follow along in their own Bibles.

—Step 3—
Guiding the Discussion
(The Core of Your Time)

This is where the inductive process comes alive through discussion of the six questions. The questions in this study are designed to spark meaningful interaction and lead to personal application. Guide your group thoughtfully through each question, drawing out insights and connecting the truths to daily life.

1. **Ask the First Question, Then Pause:** Begin with Question #1. Once you've asked it, be comfortable with silence. Perhaps say, "Take several seconds to think about that before you answer." This creates space for thoughtful responses, not just quick ones.

2. **Listen Actively and Affirm:** As people share, listen intently.
   - Restate the comment: "I like that. In case someone didn't hear, [Name] said ..."
   - Value every contribution: "Thanks for sharing that!" or "That's really good!"
   - Engage with their thoughts: "What I hear you saying is ____" or "Can you tell me more about that?"
   - Avoid over-praising one person: Your goal is to make everyone feel equally appreciated and valued.

3. **Encourage Broader Participation:** After someone shares, invite more responses.
   - "Who can build on that thought?"
   - "Give me another answer or two that complements that answer."
   - "Does anyone else have a similar or different perspective?"
   - "What resonated most with others in the group from what was just shared?"
   - "Can someone give an example of how this principle might play out in everyday life?"
   - "How does what we just discussed shift or confirm your understanding of ____?"

4. **Navigating Getting Off Track (Gently Re-Direct):**
   Discussions can stray from the topic at hand. Have polite transition statements prepared.
   - "Let's hold on to that for the moment, but I want to hear more about that from you after our class."
   - "I'd love to hear more about that when we're done, but I want to make sure we have time for others to share on this topic right now."
   - "Thanks for sharing! Many people share the same sentiment. However, for the sake of our study, let's bring our focus back to what Jesus is saying in this specific passage."
   - "I appreciate the perspectives being shared. For the benefit of the whole group, let's bring our attention back to our current question on [mention relevant Matthew passage/topic]."
   - Remember the "table" concept: "That's a really interesting question, can we table that and come back to it after the study or next week?"

5. **Address Difficult Dynamics:**
   - If someone is dominating, use phrases like: "Thanks for that, [Name]! Let's hear from someone else on this."
   - If someone is consistently silent, offer gentle invitations: "Before we move on, [Name], did anything from this passage particularly stand out to you?" (Avoid putting them on the spot with direct questions they might not be ready to answer publicly.)
   - If a comment is biblically inaccurate, acknowledge their sharing, then gently pivot back to the text: "Thanks for that perspective. When we look closely at the context of [relevant Matthew passage], we see that..."

—Step 4—
Seamlessly Transitioning Between Questions
(Guiding the Inductive Flow)

Your study guide's questions are intentionally designed to progress from observation to interpretation to application. Your role is to guide the group smoothly through this flow.

- **Connect to the Previous Answer:** After a group member has shared an insight on one question, bridge it to the next. For example, in Lesson #4 ("Unveiling the Heart's Hidden Depths"), after discussing "The Spectrum of Anger" (Question #3) and the seriousness of anger: "That's a powerful discussion about the seriousness of anger in God's eyes. Knowing how deep anger can go, how does Jesus immediately emphasize the importance of swift reconciliation and apology in verse 25, as asked in "The Urgency of Reconciliation" (Question #4)?

- **Use Intentional Transitional Phrases:**
  - "Building on that thought, let's now consider …"
  - "Now that we've observed X, what does it mean for us?"
  - "Moving from what we've understood about the meaning, how does this teaching apply to our lives today?"
  - "That leads us perfectly into our next question, which focuses on …"

- **Refer to the Inductive Process:** "We've spent some good time observing the details of this text; now let's move into interpreting what it truly means." Or, "After interpreting this profound passage, how can we actively apply its truths in our daily lives?"

- **Briefly Summarize if Necessary:** If the discussion on a question was extensive, a quick summary can provide a good launchpad: "So, we've established that Jesus is calling us to a deeper righteousness than mere external adherence to the law, even down to our thoughts. With that in mind, let's look at Matthew 5:31-37 (Lesson #5) and consider how this same deep commitment applies to 'The Foundation of Marriage: Fidelity and Truth-Telling.'"

—Step 5—
Fostering Deeper Application
(Moving Beyond Hearing to Doing)

Application is where biblical truth transforms lives. Encourage your group to go beyond simply answering the application questions and to truly do them.

- **Encourage Specificity:** Push beyond generic answers. After an application question, like in Lesson #9, "Confronting Our Anxieties" ("Share one of your current worries with the group..."), you might ask a follow-up: "What's one specific, tangible step you will take this week based on Jesus' teaching about not worrying over necessities?" Encourage participants to write it down.

- **Ask "So What?" and "Now What?":** These questions shift focus from understanding to personal responsibility. For example, after discussing Matthew 5:44 (Lesson #6: "Embracing Radical Love"), instead of just "How can you love your enemies?", ask: "Who is one 'enemy' or difficult person in your life right now, and what's one practical, measurable way you can show them love this week, as suggested in the 'Extending the Hand of Love' question?"

- **Connect to Daily Life:** Help your group see how the Sermon on the Mount isn't just ancient text, but active truth for their work, family, friendships, social media interactions, and even their leisure choices. When discussing the heart issues behind anger or lust in Matthew 5:21-30 (Lesson #4), ask how these principles apply to online comments or media consumption.

—Step 6—
Concluding the Session
(The Final 5 Minutes)

The closing moments of your study are key for solidifying the week's learning and providing a clear call to action. Use this time intentionally to discuss and utilize the prayer prompt, bringing the session to a meaningful conclusion.

1. **Read the Conclusion:** Read aloud the "Conclusion" provided in the lesson. Your conclusions are designed to "summarize key takeaways," helping to solidify the learning.

2. **Lead the Prayer Prompt:** Use the "Prayer Prompt" to guide the group in prayer. This is a vital time for individuals to respond to God's Word in worship, confession, commitment, and seeking His power for application.

3. **Encourage Continued Engagement:** Remind the group to continue reflecting on the lesson and praying for one another throughout the week. Reinforce the importance of preparing for the next lesson.

Remember Your True Purpose: Transformation, Not Just Information

Ultimately, leading a small group Bible study isn't just about covering material or accumulating biblical knowledge. While important, the deeper, more profound purpose is transformation. You guide individuals in encountering God through His Word, allowing the Holy Spirit to reveal truth, challenge their perspectives, and inspire Christ-like living.

Keep the ultimate goal of spiritual growth and personal transformation at the forefront of your mind as you lead. Focus on the "Why": Why is this passage in the Bible? What is God revealing about Himself through it? What is He asking of us in response? As the "Note from the Author" states, the Sermon on the Mount is "Jesus' profound declaration of Kingdom life, offering unparalleled insights into true righteousness and what it means to genuinely follow Him."

Celebrate not just insightful answers, but also genuine attempts at vulnerability, honest questions, and tangible efforts at application. Celebrate moments when the "light bulb" goes on for someone, when a truth clicks, or when someone commits to a new step of obedience. By applying the principles we've discussed, you'll foster a vibrant and enriching environment where God's Word can profoundly impact lives, transforming hearts and minds through His truth.

Clay's Bio

Clay Gentry is the preacher at the Jackson Heights Church of Christ in Columbia, Tennessee. He shares his life with his wife of 25 years, Shelly, a reading specialist at Columbia Academy, and their four children: Isaac, Lillie, Micah, and Anna. When he's not in the pulpit, you might find him exploring an old cemetery, hiking scenic trails, repairing a car or two, or simply relaxing with a good book and a cup of coffee. *(He's also a huge Elvis fan, and secretly believes he can channel The King while singing karaoke. But that's a story for another time.)*

www.ingramcontent.com/pod-product-compliance
Lightning Source LLC
Chambersburg PA
CBHW042337040426
42447CB00017B/3467